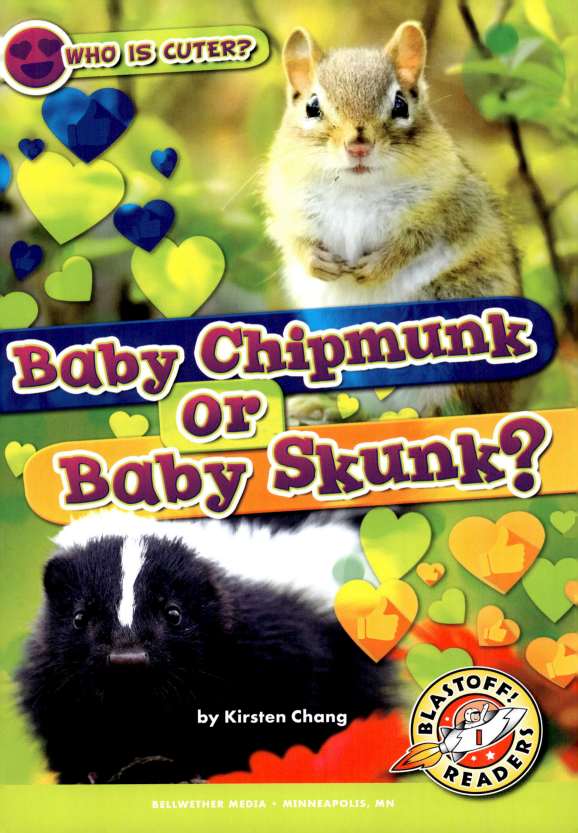

Blastoff! Readers are carefully developed by literacy experts to build reading stamina and move students toward fluency by combining standards-based content with developmentally appropriate text.

 Level 1 provides the most support through repetition of high-frequency words, light text, predictable sentence patterns, and strong visual support.

 Level 2 offers early readers a bit more challenge through varied sentences, increased text load, and text-supportive special features.

 Level 3 advances early-fluent readers toward fluency through increased text load, less reliance on photos, advancing concepts, longer sentences, and more complex special features.

★ **Blastoff! Universe**

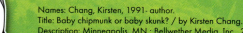

Reading Level — Grade K — Grades 1–3 — Grade 4

This edition first published in 2025 by Bellwether Media, Inc.

No part of this publication may be reproduced in whole or in part without written permission of the publisher. For information regarding permission, write to Bellwether Media, Inc., Attention: Permissions Department, 6012 Blue Circle Drive, Minnetonka, MN 55343.

Library of Congress Cataloging-in-Publication Data

Names: Chang, Kirsten, 1991- author.
Title: Baby chipmunk or baby skunk? / by Kirsten Chang.
Description: Minneapolis, MN : Bellwether Media, Inc., 2025. | Series: Blastoff! Readers: who is cuter? | Includes bibliographical references and index. | Audience term: Children | Audience term: School children | Audience: Ages 5-8 | Audience: Grades K-1 | Summary: "Developed by literacy experts for students in kindergarten through grade three, this book introduces baby chipmunks and baby skunks to young readers through leveled text and related photos"–Provided by publisher.
Identifiers: LCCN 2024035012 (print) | LCCN 2024035013 (ebook) | ISBN 9798893042238 (library binding) | ISBN 9798893044027 (paperback) | ISBN 9798893043204 (ebook)
Subjects: LCSH: Chipmunks–Infancy–Juvenile literature. | Skunks–Infancy–Juvenile literature.
Classification: LCC QL706.2 .C43 2025 (print) | LCC QL706.2 (ebook) | DDC 599.13/92–dc23/eng/20240802
LC record available at https://lccn.loc.gov/2024035012
LC ebook record available at https://lccn.loc.gov/2024035013

Text copyright © 2025 by Bellwether Media, Inc. BLASTOFF! READERS and associated logos are trademarks and/or registered trademarks of Bellwether Media, Inc.

Editor: Rachael Barnes   Designer: Andrea Schneider

Printed in the United States of America, North Mankato, MN.

Table of Contents

Pups and Kits	4
Fur and Tails	8
Day and Night	14
Who Is Cuter?	20
Glossary	22
To Learn More	23
Index	24

Pups and Kits

Baby chipmunks are often called pups. Baby skunks are called kits.

Pups and kits are both **mammals**. They have striped fur. They are cute babies!

Fur and Tails

Pups have mostly brown fur. Kits have black and white fur.

Pups have skinny tails.
Kits have fluffy tails.

These babies grow quickly. Pups stay small. Kits grow up to be much larger!

Day and Night

Pups play during the day. Kits are **nocturnal**. They play and **explore** at night.

exploring at night

Pups carry food in their big cheeks! Kits have big **claws**. They dig to find food.

Pups can run fast.
Kits can **stomp**!
Which one is cuter?

Who Is Cuter?

brown fur

big cheeks

skinny tail

Baby Chipmunk

plays during the day

carries food

runs fast

Glossary

claws

sharp, curved nails on the toes of an animal

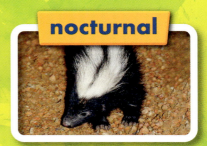

nocturnal

active at night

explore

to walk and look around to learn about a new place

stomp

to hit the ground hard with the bottom of the foot

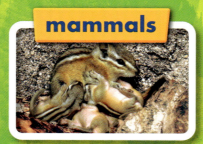

mammals

warm-blooded animals that have backbones and feed their young milk

To Learn More

AT THE LIBRARY

Chanez, Katie. *Skunk Kits in the Wild*. Minneapolis, Minn.: Jump!, 2024.

Morlock, Rachael. *Baby Backyard Animals*. Buffalo, N.Y.: PowerKids Press, 2025.

Ruby, Rex. *Inside a Chipmunk's Home*. Minneapolis, Minn.: Bearport Publishing Company, 2023.

ON THE WEB

FACTSURFER

Factsurfer.com gives you a safe, fun way to find more information.

1. Go to www.factsurfer.com.

2. Enter "baby chipmunk or baby skunk" into the search box and click 🔍.

3. Select your book cover to see a list of related content.

Index

cheeks, 16, 17
chipmunks, 4
claws, 16, 17
colors, 8
day, 14
explore, 14
food, 16
fur, 6, 8
mammals, 6
night, 14
play, 14
run, 18
size, 12
skunks, 4
stomp, 18
tails, 10, 11